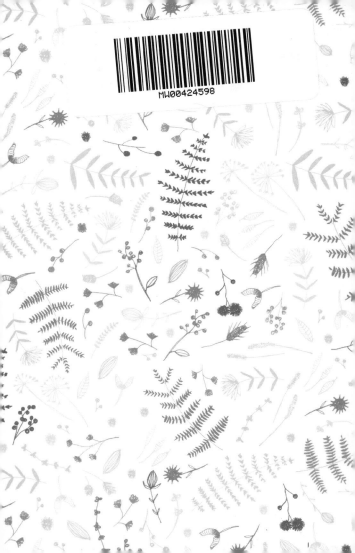

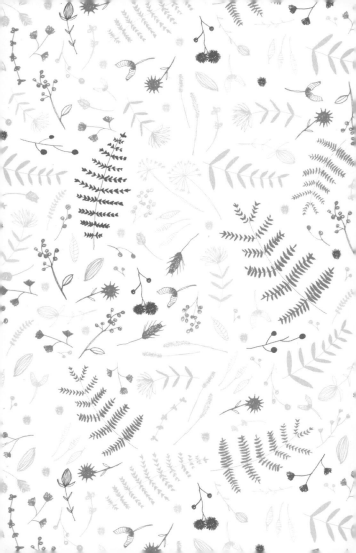

This journal belongs to

The DAILY QUESTION

⫸⫷

My 5-Year
SPIRITUAL
JOURNAL

WATERBROOK

THE DAILY QUESTION

Trade Paperback ISBN 978-0-7352-9081-5

Copyright © 2017 by WaterBrook

Cover design by Mark D. Ford; cover illustration by Nathalie Ouederni

Published in the United States by WaterBrook, an imprint of the Crown Publishing Group, a division of Penguin Random House LLC, New York.

WaterBrook® and its deer colophon are registered trademarks of Penguin Random House LLC.

Printed in China
2017—First Edition

10 9 8 7 6 5 4 3 2 1

SPECIAL SALES
Most WaterBrook books are available at special quantity discounts when purchased in bulk by corporations, organizations, and special-interest groups. Custom imprinting or excerpting can also be done to fit special needs. For information, please e-mail specialmarketscms@penguinrandomhouse.com or call 1-800-603-7051.

JANUARY

JANUARY

What New Year's resolutions
are you making this year?

20 _____ • _____

_____

_____

_____

20 _____ • _____

_____

_____

_____

20 _____ • _____

_____

_____

_____

20 _____ • _____

_____

_____

_____

20 _____ • _____

_____

_____

_____

JANUARY

What do you believe in?

20 _____ • _____

_____

_____

_____

20 _____ • _____

_____

_____

_____

20 _____ • _____

_____

_____

_____

20 _____ • _____

_____

_____

_____

20 _____ • _____

_____

_____

_____

What is God calling you to this year?

20 _____ • _____

_____

_____

_____

20 _____ • _____

_____

_____

_____

20 _____ • _____

_____

_____

_____

20 _____ • _____

_____

_____

_____

20 _____ • _____

_____

_____

_____

JANUARY

What gives you comfort right now?

20 ___ • _____

_____

_____

_____

20 ___ • _____

_____

_____

_____

20 ___ • _____

_____

_____

_____

20 ___ • _____

_____

_____

_____

20 ___ • _____

_____

_____

_____

JANUARY

When was the last time you cried?

20_____ • _____

_____

_____

_____

20_____ • _____

_____

_____

_____

20_____ • _____

_____

_____

_____

20_____ • _____

_____

_____

_____

20_____ • _____

_____

_____

_____

JANUARY

What was your favorite day this week?

20 _____ • _____

20 _____ • _____

20 _____ • _____

20 _____ • _____

20 _____ • _____

20 _____ • _____

_____

_____

_____

20 _____ • _____

_____

_____

_____

20 _____ • _____

_____

_____

_____

20 _____ • _____

_____

_____

_____

20 _____ • _____

_____

_____

_____

JANUARY

Who has encouraged you lately?

20 _____ • _____

_____

_____

_____

20 _____ • _____

_____

_____

_____

20 _____ • _____

_____

_____

_____

20 _____ • _____

_____

_____

_____

20 _____ • _____

_____

_____

_____

What experience most shaped
your faith this past year?

20 _____ • _____

_____

_____

_____

20 _____ • _____

_____

_____

_____

20 _____ • _____

_____

_____

_____

20 _____ • _____

_____

_____

_____

20 _____ • _____

_____

_____

_____

JANUARY

What are you afraid of?

20 _____ • _____

_____

_____

_____

20 _____ • _____

_____

_____

_____

20 _____ • _____

_____

_____

_____

20 _____ • _____

_____

_____

_____

20 _____ • _____

_____

_____

_____

Who do you need to forgive?

20 _____ • _____
_____
_____
_____

20 _____ • _____
_____
_____
_____

20 _____ • _____
_____
_____
_____

20 _____ • _____
_____
_____
_____

20 _____ • _____
_____
_____
_____

JANUARY

What is your most recent act of generosity?

20 _____ • _____

_____

_____

_____

20 _____ • _____

_____

_____

_____

20 _____ • _____

_____

_____

_____

20 _____ • _____

_____

_____

_____

20 _____ • _____

_____

_____

_____

JANUARY

Today I need God to _____.

20 ___ • _____
_____
_____
_____

20 ___ • _____
_____
_____
_____

20 ___ • _____
_____
_____
_____

20 ___ • _____
_____
_____
_____

20 ___ • _____
_____
_____
_____

JANUARY

How can you give grace to others this week?

20 _____ • _____

_____

_____

_____

20 _____ • _____

_____

_____

_____

20 _____ • _____

_____

_____

_____

20 _____ • _____

_____

_____

_____

20 _____ • _____

_____

_____

_____

JANUARY

What words speak hope into your life?

20 _____ • _____
_____
_____
_____

20 _____ • _____
_____
_____
_____

20 _____ • _____
_____
_____
_____

20 _____ • _____
_____
_____
_____

20 _____ • _____
_____
_____
_____

JANUARY

What do you wish were different?

20 _____ • _____

20 _____ • _____

20 _____ • _____

20 _____ • _____

20 _____ • _____

What have you had to sacrifice
to follow Jesus?

20 _____ • _____

_____

_____

_____

20 _____ • _____

_____

_____

_____

20 _____ • _____

_____

_____

_____

20 _____ • _____

_____

_____

_____

20 _____ • _____

_____

_____

_____

JANUARY

What brought you joy today?

20 _____ • _____

_____

_____

_____

20 _____ • _____

_____

_____

_____

20 _____ • _____

_____

_____

_____

20 _____ • _____

_____

_____

_____

20 _____ • _____

_____

_____

_____

JANUARY

Regardless of your age, what do you
want to be when you grow up?

20 _____ • _____

_____

_____

_____

20 _____ • _____

_____

_____

_____

20 _____ • _____

_____

_____

_____

20 _____ • _____

_____

_____

_____

20 _____ • _____

_____

_____

_____

JANUARY

Do you feel like you make enough money?

20 ___ • _____

_____

_____

_____

20 ___ • _____

_____

_____

_____

20 ___ • _____

_____

_____

_____

20 ___ • _____

_____

_____

_____

20 ___ • _____

_____

_____

_____

JANUARY

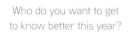

Who do you want to get
to know better this year?

20 _____ • _____
_____
_____
_____

20 _____ • _____
_____
_____
_____

20 _____ • _____
_____
_____
_____

20 _____ • _____
_____
_____
_____

20 _____ • _____
_____
_____
_____

20 _____ • _____

_____

_____

_____

20 _____ • _____

_____

_____

_____

20 _____ • _____

_____

_____

_____

20 _____ • _____

_____

_____

_____

20 _____ • _____

_____

_____

_____

How can you restore a relationship
with someone this week?

20 _____ • _____

_____

_____

_____

20 _____ • _____

_____

_____

_____

20 _____ • _____

_____

_____

_____

20 _____ • _____

_____

_____

_____

20 _____ • _____

_____

_____

_____

JANUARY

What are you praying for right now?

20 _____ • _____

_____

_____

_____

20 _____ • _____

_____

_____

_____

20 _____ • _____

_____

_____

_____

20 _____ • _____

_____

_____

_____

20 _____ • _____

_____

_____

_____

How do you relax after a stressful day?

20 _____ • _____

_____

_____

_____

20 _____ • _____

_____

_____

_____

20 _____ • _____

_____

_____

_____

20 _____ • _____

_____

_____

_____

20 _____ • _____

_____

_____

_____

JANUARY

What three words would people
use to describe you?

20 ____ • _____

_____

_____

_____

20 ____ • _____

_____

_____

_____

20 ____ • _____

_____

_____

_____

20 ____ • _____

_____

_____

_____

20 ____ • _____

_____

_____

_____

JANUARY

What new skill would you like to learn?

20 ___ • _____

_____

_____

_____

20 ___ • _____

_____

_____

_____

20 ___ • _____

_____

_____

_____

20 ___ • _____

_____

_____

_____

20 ___ • _____

_____

_____

_____

JANUARY

What song can you not stop singing?

20 _____ • _____

_____

_____

_____

20 _____ • _____

_____

_____

_____

20 _____ • _____

_____

_____

_____

20 _____ • _____

_____

_____

_____

20 _____ • _____

_____

_____

_____

JANUARY

What are you thankful for?

20 _____ • _____

_____

_____

_____

20 _____ • _____

_____

_____

_____

20 _____ • _____

_____

_____

_____

20 _____ • _____

_____

_____

_____

20 _____ • _____

_____

_____

_____

JANUARY

The best hour of today was _____. Why?

20 ___ • _____

_____

_____

_____

20 ___ • _____

_____

_____

_____

20 ___ • _____

_____

_____

_____

20 ___ • _____

_____

_____

_____

20 ___ • _____

_____

_____

_____

Who provides spiritual leadership in your life?

20 _____ • _____

_____

_____

_____

20 _____ • _____

_____

_____

_____

20 _____ • _____

_____

_____

_____

20 _____ • _____

_____

_____

_____

20 _____ • _____

_____

_____

_____

FEBRUARY

20 _____ • _____

_____

_____

_____

20 _____ • _____

_____

_____

_____

20 _____ • _____

_____

_____

_____

20 _____ • _____

_____

_____

_____

20 _____ • _____

_____

_____

_____

FEBRUARY

What questions are you asking
yourself these days?

20 _____ • _____

_____

_____

_____

20 _____ • _____

_____

_____

_____

20 _____ • _____

_____

_____

_____

20 _____ • _____

_____

_____

_____

20 _____ • _____

_____

_____

_____

FEBRUARY

What has recently made you laugh?

20 ___ • _____

_____

_____

_____

20 ___ • _____

_____

_____

_____

20 ___ • _____

_____

_____

_____

20 ___ • _____

_____

_____

_____

20 ___ • _____

_____

_____

_____

FEBRUARY

Which character from television, literature,
or a movie are you most like?

20 _____ • _____

20 _____ • _____

20 _____ • _____

20 _____ • _____

20 _____ • _____

What can you do to expand your cultural
awareness or experiences?

20 _____ • _____

_____

_____

_____

20 _____ • _____

_____

_____

_____

20 _____ • _____

_____

_____

_____

20 _____ • _____

_____

_____

_____

20 _____ • _____

_____

_____

_____

FEBRUARY

What do you have too much of?

20 _____ • _____

_____

_____

_____

20 _____ • _____

_____

_____

_____

20 _____ • _____

_____

_____

_____

20 _____ • _____

_____

_____

_____

20 _____ • _____

_____

_____

_____

When was the last time you felt fully rested?

20 _____ • _____

_____

_____

_____

20 _____ • _____

_____

_____

_____

20 _____ • _____

_____

_____

_____

20 _____ • _____

_____

_____

_____

20 _____ • _____

_____

_____

_____

FEBRUARY

What do you want to accomplish today?

20 _____ • _____

_____

_____

_____

20 _____ • _____

_____

_____

_____

20 _____ • _____

_____

_____

_____

20 _____ • _____

_____

_____

_____

20 _____ • _____

_____

_____

_____

Where did you most recently
encounter unexpected beauty?

20 _____ • _____

_____

_____

_____

20 _____ • _____

_____

_____

_____

20 _____ • _____

_____

_____

_____

20 _____ • _____

_____

_____

_____

20 _____ • _____

_____

_____

_____

FEBRUARY

What needs to be invented?

20 ___ • _____

_____

_____

20 ___ • _____

_____

_____

20 ___ • _____

_____

_____

20 ___ • _____

_____

_____

20 ___ • _____

_____

_____

FEBRUARY

What is the next book you want
to read but haven't started yet?

20 ___ • _____

_____

_____

_____

20 ___ • _____

_____

_____

_____

20 ___ • _____

_____

_____

_____

20 ___ • _____

_____

_____

_____

20 ___ • _____

_____

_____

_____

FEBRUARY

What are you celebrating today?

20 _____ • _____

_____

_____

_____

20 _____ • _____

_____

_____

_____

20 _____ • _____

_____

_____

_____

20 _____ • _____

_____

_____

_____

20 _____ • _____

_____

_____

_____

20 ____ • _____

_____

_____

_____

20 ____ • _____

_____

_____

_____

20 ____ • _____

_____

_____

_____

20 ____ • _____

_____

_____

_____

20 ____ • _____

_____

_____

_____

FEBRUARY

What compliment has someone
given you that meant a lot?

20 ___ • _____

_____

_____

_____

20 ___ • _____

_____

_____

_____

20 ___ • _____

_____

_____

_____

20 ___ • _____

_____

_____

_____

20 ___ • _____

_____

_____

_____

How have you stepped
out of your comfort zone?

20 _____ • _____
_____
_____
_____

20 _____ • _____
_____
_____
_____

20 _____ • _____
_____
_____
_____

20 _____ • _____
_____
_____
_____

20 _____ • _____
_____
_____
_____

Where do you see yourself in five years?

20 _____ • _____

_____

_____

_____

20 _____ • _____

_____

_____

_____

20 _____ • _____

_____

_____

_____

20 _____ • _____

_____

_____

_____

20 _____ • _____

_____

_____

_____

What misconceptions do people have about you?

20 _____ • _____

_____

_____

_____

20 _____ • _____

_____

_____

_____

20 _____ • _____

_____

_____

_____

20 _____ • _____

_____

_____

_____

20 _____ • _____

_____

_____

_____

FEBRUARY

Do you believe God is good? Why or why not?

20 ____ • _____

_____

_____

20 ____ • _____

_____

_____

20 ____ • _____

_____

_____

20 ____ • _____

_____

_____

20 ____ • _____

_____

_____

FEBRUARY

How can you give yourself grace tomorrow?

20 ___ • _____

_____

_____

_____

20 ___ • _____

_____

_____

_____

20 ___ • _____

_____

_____

_____

20 ___ • _____

_____

_____

_____

20 ___ • _____

_____

_____

_____

FEBRUARY

What do you wish you had more of?

20 _____ • _____

_____

_____

_____

20 _____ • _____

_____

_____

_____

20 _____ • _____

_____

_____

_____

20 _____ • _____

_____

_____

_____

20 _____ • _____

_____

_____

_____

FEBRUARY

What have you idolized lately?

20 _____ • _____

_____

_____

_____

20 _____ • _____

_____

_____

_____

20 _____ • _____

_____

_____

_____

20 _____ • _____

_____

_____

_____

20 _____ • _____

_____

_____

_____

FEBRUARY

If you could slip away from your responsibilities
for a day, what would you do?

20 _____ • _____

_____

_____

_____

20 _____ • _____

_____

_____

_____

20 _____ • _____

_____

_____

_____

20 _____ • _____

_____

_____

_____

20 _____ • _____

_____

_____

_____

FEBRUARY

Where do you find joy?

20 ___ • _____

_____

_____

_____

20 ___ • _____

_____

_____

_____

20 ___ • _____

_____

_____

_____

20 ___ • _____

_____

_____

_____

20 ___ • _____

_____

_____

_____

FEBRUARY

How has God tangibly shown
love to you this week?

20 _____ • _____

_____

_____

20 _____ • _____

_____

_____

20 _____ • _____

_____

_____

20 _____ • _____

_____

_____

20 _____ • _____

_____

_____

If you could change one relationship,
which one would it be?

20 _____ • _____

_____

_____

_____

20 _____ • _____

_____

_____

_____

20 _____ • _____

_____

_____

_____

20 _____ • _____

_____

_____

_____

20 _____ • _____

_____

_____

_____

FEBRUARY

Who needs you today?

20 _____ • _____

_____

_____

_____

20 _____ • _____

_____

_____

_____

20 _____ • _____

_____

_____

_____

20 _____ • _____

_____

_____

_____

20 _____ • _____

_____

_____

_____

What is your biggest question
for God right now?

20 _____ • _____

_____

_____

_____

20 _____ • _____

_____

_____

_____

20 _____ • _____

_____

_____

_____

20 _____ • _____

_____

_____

_____

_____

20 _____ • _____

_____

_____

_____

FEBRUARY

What do you need a break from?

20 _____ • _____

_____

_____

20 _____ • _____

_____

_____

20 _____ • _____

_____

_____

20 _____ • _____

_____

_____

20 _____ • _____

_____

_____

FEBRUARY

What did/will you do with this extra day?

20 _____ • _____

_____

_____

_____

20 _____ • _____

_____

_____

_____

20 _____ • _____

_____

_____

_____

20 _____ • _____

_____

_____

_____

20 _____ • _____

_____

_____

_____

MARCH

MARCH

What is the last risk you took?

20 _____ • _____

_____

_____

_____

20 _____ • _____

_____

_____

_____

20 _____ • _____

_____

_____

_____

20 _____ • _____

_____

_____

_____

20 _____ • _____

_____

_____

_____

MARCH

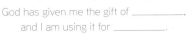

God has given me the gift of _____,
and I am using it for _____.

20 ____ • _____

_____

_____

_____

20 ____ • _____

_____

_____

_____

20 ____ • _____

_____

_____

_____

20 ____ • _____

_____

_____

_____

20 ____ • _____

_____

_____

_____

MARCH

Today was _____.

20 ____ • _____

_____

_____

_____

20 ____ • _____

_____

_____

_____

20 ____ • _____

_____

_____

_____

20 ____ • _____

_____

_____

_____

20 ____ • _____

_____

_____

_____

MARCH

What truth from God about yourself
do you need to start believing?

20 _____ • _____

_____

_____

_____

20 _____ • _____

_____

_____

_____

20 _____ • _____

_____

_____

_____

20 _____ • _____

_____

_____

_____

20 _____ • _____

_____

_____

_____

20 _____ • _____

_____

_____

_____

20 _____ • _____

_____

_____

_____

20 _____ • _____

_____

_____

_____

20 _____ • _____

_____

_____

_____

20 _____ • _____

_____

_____

_____

MARCH

How can you care for someone
who is vulnerable?

20 _____ • _____

_____

_____

20 _____ • _____

_____

_____

20 _____ • _____

_____

_____

20 _____ • _____

_____

_____

20 _____ • _____

_____

_____

Which character from television,
literature, or a movie would you like
to be best friends with?

20 _____ • _____

_____

_____

_____

20 _____ • _____

_____

_____

_____

20 _____ • _____

_____

_____

_____

20 _____ • _____

_____

_____

_____

20 _____ • _____

_____

_____

_____

MARCH

What's on your to-do list today?

20 _____ • _____

_____

_____

_____

20 _____ • _____

_____

_____

_____

20 _____ • _____

_____

_____

_____

20 _____ • _____

_____

_____

_____

20 _____ • _____

_____

_____

_____

Are you giving anything up for Lent this year?

20 _____ • _____

_____

_____

_____

20 _____ • _____

_____

_____

_____

20 _____ • _____

_____

_____

_____

20 _____ • _____

_____

_____

_____

20 _____ • _____

_____

_____

_____

MARCH

What Old Testament story or
verse speaks to you?

20 _____ • _____

_____

_____

_____

20 _____ • _____

_____

_____

_____

20 _____ • _____

_____

_____

_____

20 _____ • _____

_____

_____

_____

20 _____ • _____

_____

_____

_____

What Bible verse will you
meditate on several times today?

20 _____ • _____

_____

_____

_____

20 _____ • _____

_____

_____

_____

20 _____ • _____

_____

_____

_____

20 _____ • _____

_____

_____

_____

20 _____ • _____

_____

_____

_____

MARCH

What is your mission?

20 ___ • _____

_____

_____

_____

20 ___ • _____

_____

_____

_____

20 ___ • _____

_____

_____

_____

20 ___ • _____

_____

_____

_____

20 ___ • _____

_____

_____

_____

What do you wish you had the courage to do?

20 _____ • _____

_____

_____

_____

20 _____ • _____

_____

_____

_____

20 _____ • _____

_____

_____

_____

20 _____ • _____

_____

_____

_____

20 _____ • _____

_____

_____

_____

MARCH

What's one thing you can do
today to grow your faith?

20 _____ • _____

_____

_____

_____

20 _____ • _____

_____

_____

_____

20 _____ • _____

_____

_____

_____

20 _____ • _____

_____

_____

_____

20 _____ • _____

_____

_____

_____

MARCH

What are you looking forward to?

20 _____ • _____

20 _____ • _____

20 _____ • _____

20 _____ • _____

20 _____ • _____

MARCH

How has God shown up in your
life today or this week?

20 _____ • _____

_____

_____

_____

20 _____ • _____

_____

_____

_____

20 _____ • _____

_____

_____

_____

20 _____ • _____

_____

_____

_____

20 _____ • _____

_____

_____

_____

If you could spend three months living
anywhere in the world, where would that be?

20 ___ • _____

_____

_____

_____

20 ___ • _____

_____

_____

_____

20 ___ • _____

_____

_____

_____

20 ___ • _____

_____

_____

_____

20 ___ • _____

_____

_____

_____

MARCH

Who do you often ignore,
and how can you change that?

20 _____ • _____

_____

_____

_____

20 _____ • _____

_____

_____

_____

20 _____ • _____

_____

_____

_____

20 _____ • _____

_____

_____

_____

20 _____ • _____

_____

_____

_____

20 _____ • _____

_____

_____

_____

20 _____ • _____

_____

_____

_____

20 _____ • _____

_____

_____

_____

20 _____ • _____

_____

_____

_____

20 _____ • _____

_____

_____

_____

MARCH

What's your biggest obstacle right now?

20 _____ • _____

_____

_____

20 _____ • _____

_____

_____

20 _____ • _____

_____

_____

20 _____ • _____

_____

_____

20 _____ • _____

_____

_____

MARCH

How does Jesus love people through you?

20 _____ • _____

_____

_____

_____

20 _____ • _____

_____

_____

_____

20 _____ • _____

_____

_____

_____

20 _____ • _____

_____

_____

_____

20 _____ • _____

_____

_____

_____

MARCH

Is there someone you can pray for
who you've never prayed for before?

20 _____ • _____

_____

_____

_____

20 _____ • _____

_____

_____

_____

20 _____ • _____

_____

_____

_____

20 _____ • _____

_____

_____

_____

20 _____ • _____

_____

_____

_____

What do you not want to talk about?

20 _____ • _____

_____

_____

_____

20 _____ • _____

_____

_____

_____

20 _____ • _____

_____

_____

_____

20 _____ • _____

_____

_____

_____

20 _____ • _____

_____

_____

_____

MARCH

Are you a leader or a follower?

20 _____ • _____

_____

_____

20 _____ • _____

_____

_____

20 _____ • _____

_____

_____

20 _____ • _____

_____

_____

20 _____ • _____

_____

_____

MARCH

What is something brave
you have done this week?

20 _____ • _____

_____

_____

_____

20 _____ • _____

_____

_____

_____

20 _____ • _____

_____

_____

_____

20 _____ • _____

_____

_____

_____

20 _____ • _____

_____

_____

_____

Do you have trouble being humble?

20 _____ • _____

_____

_____

_____

20 _____ • _____

_____

_____

_____

20 _____ • _____

_____

_____

_____

20 _____ • _____

_____

_____

_____

20 _____ • _____

_____

_____

_____

MARCH

Who are you thankful for?

20 _____ • _____

_____

_____

_____

20 _____ • _____

_____

_____

_____

20 _____ • _____

_____

_____

_____

20 _____ • _____

_____

_____

_____

20 _____ • _____

_____

_____

_____

MARCH

What five words could describe this day?

20 _____ • _____

_____

_____

_____

20 _____ • _____

_____

_____

_____

20 _____ • _____

_____

_____

_____

20 _____ • _____

_____

_____

_____

20 _____ • _____

_____

_____

_____

What is one of your traditions
during the Easter season?

20 _____ • _____

_____

_____

_____

20 _____ • _____

_____

_____

_____

20 _____ • _____

_____

_____

_____

20 _____ • _____

_____

_____

_____

20 _____ • _____

_____

_____

_____

MARCH

What don't you have time for?

30

20 _____ • _____

_____

_____

_____

20 _____ • _____

_____

_____

_____

20 _____ • _____

_____

_____

_____

20 _____ • _____

_____

_____

_____

20 _____ • _____

_____

_____

_____

MARCH

What surprised you recently?

20 _____ • _____

_____

_____

_____

20 _____ • _____

_____

_____

_____

20 _____ • _____

_____

_____

_____

20 _____ • _____

_____

_____

_____

20 _____ • _____

_____

_____

_____

APRIL

APRIL

Were you "foolish" today? Was it intentional?
Would you do it again?

20 _____ • _____

_____

_____

_____

20 _____ • _____

_____

_____

_____

20 _____ • _____

_____

_____

_____

20 _____ • _____

_____

_____

_____

20 _____ • _____

_____

_____

_____

APRIL

What small goal would you like
to accomplish this week?

20 _____ • _____

_____

_____

_____

20 _____ • _____

_____

_____

_____

20 _____ • _____

_____

_____

_____

20 _____ • _____

_____

_____

_____

20 _____ • _____

_____

_____

_____

APRIL

What is robbing you of joy right now?

20 ___ • _____

_____

_____

_____

20 ___ • _____

_____

_____

_____

20 ___ • _____

_____

_____

_____

20 ___ • _____

_____

_____

_____

20 ___ • _____

_____

_____

_____

APRIL

For what do you need to give yourself grace?

20 _____ • _____

_____

_____

_____

20 _____ • _____

_____

_____

_____

20 _____ • _____

_____

_____

_____

20 _____ • _____

_____

_____

_____

20 _____ • _____

_____

_____

_____

Which fruit of the Spirit would your coworkers
or friends say you most embody?
(See Galatians 5:22–23.)

20 ___ • _____

_____

_____

_____

20 ___ • _____

_____

_____

_____

20 ___ • _____

_____

_____

_____

20 ___ • _____

_____

_____

_____

20 ___ • _____

_____

_____

_____

APRIL

What difficult task have you been avoiding
and why? (See Galatians 5:22–23.)

20 _____ • _____

_____

_____

_____

20 _____ • _____

_____

_____

_____

20 _____ • _____

_____

_____

_____

20 _____ • _____

_____

_____

_____

20 _____ • _____

_____

_____

_____

What is something you need to complete today?

20 ___ • _____

_____

_____

_____

20 ___ • _____

_____

_____

_____

20 ___ • _____

_____

_____

_____

20 ___ • _____

_____

_____

_____

20 ___ • _____

_____

_____

_____

APRIL

What's the last book you finished?

20 _____ • _____

_____

_____

_____

20 _____ • _____

_____

_____

_____

20 _____ • _____

_____

_____

_____

20 _____ • _____

_____

_____

_____

20 _____ • _____

_____

_____

_____

9

APRIL

What does church look like to you?

20 _____ • _____
_____
_____
_____

20 _____ • _____
_____
_____
_____

20 _____ • _____
_____
_____
_____

20 _____ • _____
_____
_____
_____

20 _____ • _____
_____
_____
_____

APRIL

What is stopping you from dreaming bigger?

20 _____ • _____

20 _____ • _____

20 _____ • _____

20 _____ • _____

20 _____ • _____

APRIL

Who do you need to reconcile with?

20 ____ • _____

_____

_____

_____

20 ____ • _____

_____

_____

_____

20 ____ • _____

_____

_____

_____

20 ____ • _____

_____

_____

_____

20 ____ • _____

_____

_____

_____

APRIL

What is one thing you'd like to remind
yourself of in five years?

20 ____ • _____

_____

_____

_____

20 ____ • _____

_____

_____

_____

20 ____ • _____

_____

_____

_____

20 ____ • _____

_____

_____

_____

20 ____ • _____

_____

_____

_____

APRIL

The last time I felt angry at God
was _____.

20 ____ • _____

_____

_____

_____

20 ____ • _____

_____

_____

_____

20 ____ • _____

_____

_____

_____

20 ____ • _____

_____

_____

_____

20 ____ • _____

_____

_____

_____

APRIL

What do you imagine heaven is like?

20 _____ • _____

_____

_____

_____

20 _____ • _____

_____

_____

_____

20 _____ • _____

_____

_____

_____

20 _____ • _____

_____

_____

_____

20 _____ • _____

_____

_____

_____

APRIL

If today were a color, what color would it be?

20 _____ • _____

_____

_____

_____

20 _____ • _____

_____

_____

_____

20 _____ • _____

_____

_____

_____

20 _____ • _____

_____

_____

_____

20 _____ • _____

_____

_____

_____

APRIL

Who do you know who needs Jesus?

20 _____ • _____

_____

_____

_____

20 _____ • _____

_____

_____

_____

20 _____ • _____

_____

_____

_____

20 _____ • _____

_____

_____

_____

20 _____ • _____

_____

_____

_____

APRIL

What made you laugh today?

20 _____ • _____

_____

_____

_____

20 _____ • _____

_____

_____

_____

20 _____ • _____

_____

_____

_____

20 _____ • _____

_____

_____

_____

20 _____ • _____

_____

_____

_____

APRIL

Who in your life needs to hear
"I love you" today?

20 ____ • _____

_____

_____

_____

20 ____ • _____

_____

_____

_____

20 ____ • _____

_____

_____

_____

20 ____ • _____

_____

_____

_____

20 ____ • _____

_____

_____

_____

Who do you most admire?

20 _____ • _____

_____

_____

_____

20 _____ • _____

_____

_____

_____

20 _____ • _____

_____

_____

_____

20 _____ • _____

_____

_____

_____

20 _____ • _____

_____

_____

_____

APRIL

Do you have good community?

20 _____ • _____

_____

_____

_____

20 _____ • _____

_____

_____

_____

20 _____ • _____

_____

_____

_____

20 _____ • _____

_____

_____

_____

20 _____ • _____

_____

_____

_____

APRIL

When did you last listen more than speak?

20 _____ • _____

_____

_____

_____

20 _____ • _____

_____

_____

_____

20 _____ • _____

_____

_____

_____

20 _____ • _____

_____

_____

_____

20 _____ • _____

_____

_____

_____

APRIL

What did you recently shrug off that
could have really bothered you if you let it?

20 ____ • _____

_____

_____

_____

20 ____ • _____

_____

_____

_____

20 ____ • _____

_____

_____

_____

20 ____ • _____

_____

_____

_____

20 ____ • _____

_____

_____

_____

APRIL

How hard are you working right now?

20 ___ • _____

_____

_____

_____

20 ___ • _____

_____

_____

_____

20 ___ • _____

_____

_____

_____

20 ___ • _____

_____

_____

_____

20 ___ • _____

_____

_____

_____

APRIL

What makes you smile?

20 _____ • _____

_____

_____

20 _____ • _____

_____

_____

20 _____ • _____

_____

_____

20 _____ • _____

_____

_____

20 _____ • _____

_____

_____

In what area of your life do you
need to be more self-aware?

20 _____ • _____

_____

_____

_____

20 _____ • _____

_____

_____

_____

20 _____ • _____

_____

_____

_____

20 _____ • _____

_____

_____

_____

20 _____ • _____

_____

_____

_____

APRIL

How will you thank someone today
who has done something for you,
no matter how small?

20 _____ • _____

_____

_____

_____

20 _____ • _____

_____

_____

_____

20 _____ • _____

_____

_____

_____

20 _____ • _____

_____

_____

_____

20 _____ • _____

_____

_____

_____

APRIL

What was the best part of today?

20 _____ • _____

_____

_____

_____

20 _____ • _____

_____

_____

_____

20 _____ • _____

_____

_____

_____

20 _____ • _____

_____

_____

_____

20 _____ • _____

_____

_____

_____

APRIL

What was the last road trip you took?

20 _____ • _____

_____

_____

_____

20 _____ • _____

_____

_____

_____

20 _____ • _____

_____

_____

_____

20 _____ • _____

_____

_____

_____

20 _____ • _____

_____

_____

_____

What is the best decision you've made recently?

20 _____ • _____

_____

_____

_____

20 _____ • _____

_____

_____

_____

20 _____ • _____

_____

_____

_____

20 _____ • _____

_____

_____

_____

20 _____ • _____

_____

_____

_____

APRIL

What is your favorite thing to do on a weekend?

20 _____ • _____

_____

_____

_____

20 _____ • _____

_____

_____

_____

20 _____ • _____

_____

_____

_____

20 _____ • _____

_____

_____

_____

20 _____ • _____

_____

_____

_____

MAY

MAY

What social issues has God
placed on your heart?

20 ____ • _____

_____

_____

_____

20 ____ • _____

_____

_____

_____

20 ____ • _____

_____

_____

_____

20 ____ • _____

_____

_____

_____

20 ____ • _____

_____

_____

_____

If you had a time machine, would you
go to the past or the future?

20 _____ • _____
_____
_____
_____

20 _____ • _____
_____
_____
_____

20 _____ • _____
_____
_____
_____

20 _____ • _____
_____
_____
_____

20 _____ • _____
_____
_____
_____

MAY

What are you trying to do in your own
strength instead of relying on God?

20 _____ • _____
_____
_____
_____

20 _____ • _____
_____
_____
_____

20 _____ • _____
_____
_____
_____

20 _____ • _____
_____
_____
_____

20 _____ • _____
_____
_____
_____

20 _____ • _____

_____

_____

_____

20 _____ • _____

_____

_____

_____

20 _____ • _____

_____

_____

_____

20 _____ • _____

_____

_____

_____

20 _____ • _____

_____

_____

_____

MAY

What's something you're avoiding?

20 ____ • _____

_____

_____

_____

20 ____ • _____

_____

_____

_____

20 ____ • _____

_____

_____

_____

20 ____ • _____

_____

_____

_____

20 ____ • _____

_____

_____

_____

If you were to write a book right now,
what would it be about?

20 _____ • _____

_____

_____

_____

20 _____ • _____

_____

_____

_____

20 _____ • _____

_____

_____

_____

20 _____ • _____

_____

_____

_____

20 _____ • _____

_____

_____

_____

MAY

How do you sense God
wants to use you today?

20 _____ • _____

_____

_____

_____

20 _____ • _____

_____

_____

_____

20 _____ • _____

_____

_____

_____

20 _____ • _____

_____

_____

_____

20 _____ • _____

_____

_____

_____

MAY

What's your simplest pleasure?

20 _____ • _____

_____

_____

_____

20 _____ • _____

_____

_____

_____

20 _____ • _____

_____

_____

_____

20 _____ • _____

_____

_____

_____

20 _____ • _____

_____

_____

_____

MAY

Who can you encourage today?

20 _____ • _____

_____

_____

20 _____ • _____

_____

_____

20 _____ • _____

_____

_____

20 _____ • _____

_____

_____

20 _____ • _____

_____

_____

10

MAY

What are you worried about?

20 _____ • _____

_____

_____

_____

20 _____ • _____

_____

_____

_____

20 _____ • _____

_____

_____

_____

20 _____ • _____

_____

_____

_____

20 _____ • _____

_____

_____

_____

MAY

What's the biggest thing you have
coming up that you have to plan for?

20 _____ • _____

_____

_____

_____

20 _____ • _____

_____

_____

_____

20 _____ • _____

_____

_____

_____

20 _____ • _____

_____

_____

_____

20 _____ • _____

_____

_____

_____

What is one spiritual goal you have?

20 _____ • _____

_____

_____

_____

20 _____ • _____

_____

_____

_____

20 _____ • _____

_____

_____

_____

20 _____ • _____

_____

_____

_____

20 _____ • _____

_____

_____

_____

How would you feel if you
saw Jesus face to face?

20 _____ • _____

_____

_____

_____

20 _____ • _____

_____

_____

_____

20 _____ • _____

_____

_____

_____

20 _____ • _____

_____

_____

_____

20 _____ • _____

_____

_____

_____

What is your favorite way to spend
a cool, rainy afternoon?

20 _____ • _____

_____

_____

_____

20 _____ • _____

_____

_____

_____

20 _____ • _____

_____

_____

_____

20 _____ • _____

_____

_____

_____

20 _____ • _____

_____

_____

_____

MAY

Where do you see growth in your life?

20 _____ • _____

_____

_____

_____

20 _____ • _____

_____

_____

_____

20 _____ • _____

_____

_____

_____

20 _____ • _____

_____

_____

_____

20 _____ • _____

_____

_____

_____

16

MAY

What is an important lesson
your parents taught you?

20 ____ • _____

_____

_____

_____

20 ____ • _____

_____

_____

_____

20 ____ • _____

_____

_____

_____

20 ____ • _____

_____

_____

_____

20 ____ • _____

_____

_____

_____

MAY

How do you enjoy showing love to others?

20 ____ • _____

_____

_____

_____

20 ____ • _____

_____

_____

_____

20 ____ • _____

_____

_____

_____

20 ____ • _____

_____

_____

_____

20 ____ • _____

_____

_____

_____

MAY

Who will you encourage today,
and how will you do it?

20 _____ • _____

_____

_____

_____

20 _____ • _____

_____

_____

_____

20 _____ • _____

_____

_____

_____

20 _____ • _____

_____

_____

_____

20 _____ • _____

_____

_____

_____

MAY

Who is your real-life hero?

20 _____ • _____

_____

_____

_____

20 _____ • _____

_____

_____

_____

20 _____ • _____

_____

_____

_____

20 _____ • _____

_____

_____

_____

20 _____ • _____

_____

_____

_____

MAY

What would make your most detestable
household chore more enjoyable or easier?

20 _____ • _____

_____

_____

_____

20 _____ • _____

_____

_____

_____

20 _____ • _____

_____

_____

_____

20 _____ • _____

_____

_____

_____

20 _____ • _____

_____

_____

_____

MAY

What wisdom would you share with
someone who is about to graduate?

20 _____ • _____

_____

_____

_____

20 _____ • _____

_____

_____

_____

20 _____ • _____

_____

_____

_____

20 _____ • _____

_____

_____

_____

20 _____ • _____

_____

_____

_____

MAY

What makes you miserable?

20 _____ • _____

_____

_____

_____

20 _____ • _____

_____

_____

_____

20 _____ • _____

_____

_____

_____

20 _____ • _____

_____

_____

_____

20 _____ • _____

_____

_____

_____

MAY

Who are you?

20 _____ • _____

_____

_____

_____

20 _____ • _____

_____

_____

_____

20 _____ • _____

_____

_____

_____

20 _____ • _____

_____

_____

_____

20 _____ • _____

_____

_____

_____

MAY

What is one nonphysical thing you'd like
to change about yourself?

20 ___ • _____

_____

_____

_____

20 ___ • _____

_____

_____

_____

20 ___ • _____

_____

_____

_____

20 ___ • _____

_____

_____

_____

20 ___ • _____

_____

_____

_____

MAY

What is one line from a favorite worship song
or hymn that you can meditate on today?

20 _____ • _____

_____

_____

_____

20 _____ • _____

_____

_____

_____

20 _____ • _____

_____

_____

_____

20 _____ • _____

_____

_____

_____

20 _____ • _____

_____

_____

_____

MAY

What is something you're grateful for
that other people might find silly?

20 ___ • _____

_____

_____

_____

20 ___ • _____

_____

_____

_____

20 ___ • _____

_____

_____

_____

20 ___ • _____

_____

_____

_____

20 ___ • _____

_____

_____

_____

MAY

The best thing about
today was _____.

20 _____ • _____

_____

_____

_____

20 _____ • _____

_____

_____

_____

20 _____ • _____

_____

_____

_____

20 _____ • _____

_____

_____

_____

20 _____ • _____

_____

_____

_____

When did you have to be honest,
even though it wasn't easy?

20 _____ • _____

_____

_____

_____

20 _____ • _____

_____

_____

_____

20 _____ • _____

_____

_____

_____

20 _____ • _____

_____

_____

_____

20 _____ • _____

_____

_____

_____

MAY

What do you have to lose?

20 ___ • _____

_____

_____

_____

20 ___ • _____

_____

_____

_____

20 ___ • _____

_____

_____

_____

20 ___ • _____

_____

_____

_____

20 ___ • _____

_____

_____

_____

What question would you ask
someone who has had a strong
faith for several decades?

20 _____ • _____

_____

_____

_____

20 _____ • _____

_____

_____

_____

20 _____ • _____

_____

_____

_____

20 _____ • _____

_____

_____

_____

20 _____ • _____

_____

_____

_____

MAY

What are you passionate about?

20 _____ • _____

_____

_____

_____

20 _____ • _____

_____

_____

_____

20 _____ • _____

_____

_____

_____

20 _____ • _____

_____

_____

_____

20 _____ • _____

_____

_____

_____

JUNE

JUNE

Which fruit of the Spirit
do you most need today?
(See Galatians 5:22–23.)

20 _____ • _____

_____

_____

20 _____ • _____

_____

_____

20 _____ • _____

_____

_____

20 _____ • _____

_____

_____

20 _____ • _____

_____

_____

What are you waiting for an answer about?

20 _____ • _____

_____

_____

_____

20 _____ • _____

_____

_____

_____

20 _____ • _____

_____

_____

_____

20 _____ • _____

_____

_____

_____

20 _____ • _____

_____

_____

_____

JUNE

What Bible verse is meaningful to you?

20 _____ • _____

_____

_____

_____

20 _____ • _____

_____

_____

_____

20 _____ • _____

_____

_____

_____

20 _____ • _____

_____

_____

_____

20 _____ • _____

_____

_____

_____

JUNE

What is your goal for this summer?

20 _____ • _____

_____

_____

_____

20 _____ • _____

_____

_____

_____

20 _____ • _____

_____

_____

_____

20 _____ • _____

_____

_____

_____

20 _____ • _____

_____

_____

_____

JUNE

What happened recently that you
are proud of or happy about?

20 _____ • _____

_____

_____

_____

20 _____ • _____

_____

_____

_____

20 _____ • _____

_____

_____

_____

20 _____ • _____

_____

_____

_____

20 _____ • _____

_____

_____

_____

JUNE

What do you need help with?

20 _____ • _____
_____
_____
_____

20 _____ • _____
_____
_____
_____

20 _____ • _____
_____
_____
_____

20 _____ • _____
_____
_____
_____

20 _____ • _____
_____
_____
_____

JUNE

Other than Jesus, who from the Bible
would you like to have dinner with?

20 ___ • _____

_____

_____

_____

20 ___ • _____

_____

_____

_____

20 ___ • _____

_____

_____

_____

20 ___ • _____

_____

_____

_____

20 ___ • _____

_____

_____

_____

What has someone said to you
that was especially encouraging?

20 _____ • _____

_____

_____

_____

20 _____ • _____

_____

_____

_____

20 _____ • _____

_____

_____

_____

20 _____ • _____

_____

_____

_____

20 _____ • _____

_____

_____

_____

JUNE

What is your weirdest fear?

20 _____ • _____

_____

_____

_____

20 _____ • _____

_____

_____

_____

20 _____ • _____

_____

_____

_____

20 _____ • _____

_____

_____

_____

20 _____ • _____

_____

_____

_____

JUNE

To what is God calling you to give
generously of your time or money?

20 ____ • _____

_____

_____

_____

20 ____ • _____

_____

_____

_____

20 ____ • _____

_____

_____

_____

20 ____ • _____

_____

_____

_____

20 ____ • _____

_____

_____

_____

JUNE

If you were in control of _____,
things would be different. How?

20 ____ • _____

_____

_____

_____

20 ____ • _____

_____

_____

_____

20 ____ • _____

_____

_____

_____

20 ____ • _____

_____

_____

_____

20 ____ • _____

_____

_____

_____

In what way has God
shown Himself faithful recently?

20 _____ • _____

_____

_____

_____

20 _____ • _____

_____

_____

_____

20 _____ • _____

_____

_____

_____

20 _____ • _____

_____

_____

_____

20 _____ • _____

_____

_____

_____

JUNE

How do you best receive love?

13

20 _____ • _____

_____

_____

_____

20 _____ • _____

_____

_____

_____

20 _____ • _____

_____

_____

_____

20 _____ • _____

_____

_____

_____

20 _____ • _____

_____

_____

_____

JUNE

Who is Jesus to you?

20 _____ • _____

_____

_____

_____

20 _____ • _____

_____

_____

_____

20 _____ • _____

_____

_____

_____

20 _____ • _____

_____

_____

_____

20 _____ • _____

_____

_____

_____

JUNE

Where do you go to find peace?

20 _____ • _____

_____

_____

_____

20 _____ • _____

_____

_____

_____

20 _____ • _____

_____

_____

_____

20 _____ • _____

_____

_____

_____

20 _____ • _____

_____

_____

_____

JUNE

What prayer feels unanswered?

20 _____ • _____

_____

_____

_____

20 _____ • _____

_____

_____

_____

20 _____ • _____

_____

_____

_____

20 _____ • _____

_____

_____

_____

20 _____ • _____

_____

_____

_____

JUNE

How can you help a friend today?

20 _____ • _____

_____

_____

_____

20 _____ • _____

_____

_____

_____

20 _____ • _____

_____

_____

_____

20 _____ • _____

_____

_____

_____

20 _____ • _____

_____

_____

_____

JUNE

What rut are you in?

20 ___ • _____

_____

_____

_____

20 ___ • _____

_____

_____

_____

20 ___ • _____

_____

_____

_____

20 ___ • _____

_____

_____

_____

20 ___ • _____

_____

_____

_____

JUNE

How is God redeeming your broken story?

20 _____ • _____

_____

_____

_____

20 _____ • _____

_____

_____

_____

20 _____ • _____

_____

_____

_____

20 _____ • _____

_____

_____

_____

20 _____ • _____

_____

_____

_____

JUNE

What's your favorite hymn?

20 _____ • _____

_____

_____

_____

20 _____ • _____

_____

_____

_____

20 _____ • _____

_____

_____

_____

20 _____ • _____

_____

_____

_____

20 _____ • _____

_____

_____

_____

JUNE

What do you do to de-stress?

20 _____ • _____

_____

_____

_____

20 _____ • _____

_____

_____

_____

20 _____ • _____

_____

_____

_____

20 _____ • _____

_____

_____

_____

20 _____ • _____

_____

_____

_____

If you could change one thing
about today, what would it be?

20 ___ • _____

_____

_____

_____

20 ___ • _____

_____

_____

_____

20 ___ • _____

_____

_____

_____

20 ___ • _____

_____

_____

_____

20 ___ • _____

_____

_____

_____

JUNE

What should you get rid of soon?

20 ____ • _____

_____

_____

_____

20 ____ • _____

_____

_____

_____

20 ____ • _____

_____

_____

_____

20 ____ • _____

_____

_____

_____

20 ____ • _____

_____

_____

_____

JUNE

What one truth about God
would you share with a five-year-old?

20 _____ • _____

_____

_____

_____

20 _____ • _____

_____

_____

_____

20 _____ • _____

_____

_____

_____

20 _____ • _____

_____

_____

_____

20 _____ • _____

_____

_____

_____

JUNE

Which character from television, literature,
or a movie do you wish you were more like?

20 _____ • _____

_____

_____

_____

20 _____ • _____

_____

_____

_____

20 _____ • _____

_____

_____

_____

20 _____ • _____

_____

_____

_____

20 _____ • _____

_____

_____

_____

What can you do to be more sensitive
to hearing God's voice?

20 _____ • _____

_____

_____

_____

20 _____ • _____

_____

_____

_____

20 _____ • _____

_____

_____

_____

20 _____ • _____

_____

_____

_____

20 _____ • _____

_____

_____

_____

JUNE

What is keeping you from doing
what you really want to do?

20 ____ • _____

_____

_____

_____

20 ____ • _____

_____

_____

_____

20 ____ • _____

_____

_____

_____

20 ____ • _____

_____

_____

_____

20 ____ • _____

_____

_____

_____

What in Scripture are you
grappling with these days?

20 _____ • _____

_____

_____

_____

20 _____ • _____

_____

_____

_____

20 _____ • _____

_____

_____

_____

20 _____ • _____

_____

_____

_____

20 _____ • _____

_____

_____

_____

JUNE

When you walked through a hard season,
what did someone do that was uplifting?

20 ____ • _____

_____

_____

_____

20 ____ • _____

_____

_____

_____

20 ____ • _____

_____

_____

_____

20 ____ • _____

_____

_____

_____

20 ____ • _____

_____

_____

_____

What do you wish you would have
known about God ten years ago?

20 _____ • _____

_____

_____

_____

20 _____ • _____

_____

_____

_____

20 _____ • _____

_____

_____

_____

20 _____ • _____

_____

_____

_____

20 _____ • _____

_____

_____

_____

JULY

JULY

If you could start today over, would you?

20 ____ • _____

_____

_____

_____

20 ____ • _____

_____

_____

_____

20 ____ • _____

_____

_____

_____

20 ____ • _____

_____

_____

_____

20 ____ • _____

_____

_____

_____

JULY

If you could travel through time
to one Bible story, which one
would you like to see in person?

20 _____ • _____

_____

_____

20 _____ • _____

_____

_____

20 _____ • _____

_____

_____

20 _____ • _____

_____

_____

20 _____ • _____

_____

_____

JULY

Who do you feel closest to?

20 _____ • _____

_____

_____

_____

20 _____ • _____

_____

_____

_____

20 _____ • _____

_____

_____

_____

20 _____ • _____

_____

_____

_____

20 _____ • _____

_____

_____

_____

JULY

What problem do you need help solving?

20 ___ • _____

_____

_____

_____

20 ___ • _____

_____

_____

_____

20 ___ • _____

_____

_____

_____

20 ___ • _____

_____

_____

_____

20 ___ • _____

_____

_____

_____

5

How have you seen God's
glory in nature recently?

20 ___ • _____
_____
_____
_____

20 ___ • _____
_____
_____
_____

20 ___ • _____
_____
_____
_____

20 ___ • _____
_____
_____
_____

20 ___ • _____
_____
_____
_____

JULY

I wish I were more _____.

20 ____ • _____
_____
_____
_____

20 ____ • _____
_____
_____
_____

20 ____ • _____
_____
_____
_____

20 ____ • _____
_____
_____
_____

20 ____ • _____
_____
_____
_____

What mundane aspect of your
life are you thankful for?

20 ____ • _____

_____

_____

_____

20 ____ • _____

_____

_____

_____

20 ____ • _____

_____

_____

_____

20 ____ • _____

_____

_____

_____

20 ____ • _____

_____

_____

_____

JULY

What destination is
your dream vacation and why?

20 _____ • _____

_____

_____

_____

20 _____ • _____

_____

_____

_____

20 _____ • _____

_____

_____

_____

20 _____ • _____

_____

_____

_____

20 _____ • _____

_____

_____

_____

How have you experienced God's providence?

20 _____ • _____

_____

_____

_____

20 _____ • _____

_____

_____

_____

20 _____ • _____

_____

_____

_____

20 _____ • _____

_____

_____

_____

20 _____ • _____

_____

_____

_____

JULY

What do you need to change
your attitude about today?

20 ____ • _____

_____

_____

_____

20 ____ • _____

_____

_____

_____

20 ____ • _____

_____

_____

_____

20 ____ • _____

_____

_____

_____

20 ____ • _____

_____

_____

_____

JULY

What are you thankful for today?

20 _____ • _____

_____

_____

_____

20 _____ • _____

_____

_____

_____

20 _____ • _____

_____

_____

_____

20 _____ • _____

_____

_____

_____

20 _____ • _____

_____

_____

_____

JULY

What was the last thing that upset you,
and how did you respond?

20 ___ • _____

20 ___ • _____

20 ___ • _____

20 ___ • _____

20 ___ • _____

What frustrates you about the Bible?

20 _____ • _____

_____

_____

_____

20 _____ • _____

_____

_____

_____

20 _____ • _____

_____

_____

_____

20 _____ • _____

_____

_____

_____

20 _____ • _____

_____

_____

_____

JULY

What do you wish you
could prevent from happening?

20 _____ • _____

_____

_____

_____

20 _____ • _____

_____

_____

_____

20 _____ • _____

_____

_____

_____

20 _____ • _____

_____

_____

_____

20 _____ • _____

_____

_____

_____

JULY

What makes you impatient?

20 ____ • _____

_____

_____

_____

20 ____ • _____

_____

_____

_____

20 ____ • _____

_____

_____

_____

20 ____ • _____

_____

_____

_____

20 ____ • _____

_____

_____

_____

JULY

Today I wish God would _____.

20 ____ • _____

_____

_____

_____

20 ____ • _____

_____

_____

_____

20 ____ • _____

_____

_____

_____

20 ____ • _____

_____

_____

_____

20 ____ • _____

_____

_____

_____

JULY

If you could have dinner
with anyone tonight, who would it be?

20 _____ • _____

_____

_____

_____

20 _____ • _____

_____

_____

_____

20 _____ • _____

_____

_____

_____

20 _____ • _____

_____

_____

_____

20 _____ • _____

_____

_____

_____

JULY

How can you make someone laugh today?

20 _____ • _____

_____

_____

_____

20 _____ • _____

_____

_____

_____

20 _____ • _____

_____

_____

_____

20 _____ • _____

_____

_____

_____

20 _____ • _____

_____

_____

_____

JULY

How have you experienced God's peace
that surpasses understanding?

20 _____ • _____

_____

_____

_____

20 _____ • _____

_____

_____

_____

20 _____ • _____

_____

_____

_____

20 _____ • _____

_____

_____

_____

20 _____ • _____

_____

_____

_____

JULY

How can you serve your community this month?

20 _____ • _____

_____

_____

_____

20 _____ • _____

_____

_____

_____

20 _____ • _____

_____

_____

_____

20 _____ • _____

_____

_____

_____

20 _____ • _____

_____

_____

_____

JULY

What did you learn this week?

20 ____ • _____

_____

_____

_____

20 ____ • _____

_____

_____

_____

20 ____ • _____

_____

_____

_____

20 ____ • _____

_____

_____

_____

20 ____ • _____

_____

_____

_____

JULY

What is something you prayed for today?

20 ___ • _____
_____
_____
_____

20 ___ • _____
_____
_____
_____

20 ___ • _____
_____
_____
_____

20 ___ • _____
_____
_____
_____

20 ___ • _____
_____
_____
_____

What could you do today
to make yourself a better person?

20 _____ • _____

_____

_____

_____

20 _____ • _____

_____

_____

_____

20 _____ • _____

_____

_____

_____

20 _____ • _____

_____

_____

_____

20 _____ • _____

_____

_____

_____

JULY

Where do you like reading your Bible?

20 _____ • _____

_____

_____

_____

20 _____ • _____

_____

_____

_____

20 _____ • _____

_____

_____

_____

20 _____ • _____

_____

_____

_____

20 _____ • _____

_____

_____

_____

JULY

What song has encouraged you?

20 _____ • _____
_____
_____
_____

20 _____ • _____
_____
_____
_____

20 _____ • _____
_____
_____
_____

20 _____ • _____
_____
_____
_____

20 _____ • _____
_____
_____
_____

JULY

Today was tough because _____.

20 ____ • _____

_____

_____

_____

20 ____ • _____

_____

_____

_____

20 ____ • _____

_____

_____

_____

20 ____ • _____

_____

_____

_____

20 ____ • _____

_____

_____

_____

What nourishes your soul?

20 _____ • _____

_____

_____

_____

20 _____ • _____

_____

_____

_____

20 _____ • _____

_____

_____

_____

20 _____ • _____

_____

_____

_____

20 _____ • _____

_____

_____

_____

JULY

The best thing about where you
live is _____.

20 ____ • _____

_____

_____

_____

20 ____ • _____

_____

_____

_____

20 ____ • _____

_____

_____

_____

20 ____ • _____

_____

_____

_____

20 ____ • _____

_____

_____

_____

20 _____ • _____

_____

_____

_____

20 _____ • _____

_____

_____

_____

20 _____ • _____

_____

_____

_____

20 _____ • _____

_____

_____

_____

20 _____ • _____

_____

_____

_____

JULY

How can you make time to be alone
with God to de-stress and receive
His love and grace today?

20 _____ • _____

_____

_____

_____

20 _____ • _____

_____

_____

_____

20 _____ • _____

_____

_____

_____

20 _____ • _____

_____

_____

_____

20 _____ • _____

_____

_____

_____

JULY

Who in the Bible do you relate to?

20 _____ • _____

_____

_____

_____

20 _____ • _____

_____

_____

_____

20 _____ • _____

_____

_____

_____

20 _____ • _____

_____

_____

_____

20 _____ • _____

_____

_____

_____

AUGUST

AUGUST

When did you last have to be brave?

20 ___ • _____

_____

_____

_____

20 ___ • _____

_____

_____

_____

20 ___ • _____

_____

_____

_____

20 ___ • _____

_____

_____

_____

20 ___ • _____

_____

_____

_____

AUGUST

What was the last sermon that made
a big impression on you?

20 _____ • _____

_____

_____

_____

20 _____ • _____

_____

_____

_____

20 _____ • _____

_____

_____

_____

20 _____ • _____

_____

_____

_____

20 _____ • _____

_____

_____

_____

When was the last time
you made someone smile?

20 ___ • _____

_____

_____

_____

20 ___ • _____

_____

_____

_____

20 ___ • _____

_____

_____

_____

20 ___ • _____

_____

_____

_____

20 ___ • _____

_____

_____

_____

AUGUST

What attribute of God are you
especially thankful for right now?

20 _____ • _____

_____

_____

_____

20 _____ • _____

_____

_____

_____

20 _____ • _____

_____

_____

_____

20 _____ • _____

_____

_____

_____

20 _____ • _____

_____

_____

_____

What action did you take today
to show someone love?

20 _____ • _____

_____

_____

_____

20 _____ • _____

_____

_____

_____

20 _____ • _____

_____

_____

_____

20 _____ • _____

_____

_____

_____

20 _____ • _____

_____

_____

_____

AUGUST

Are you proud of what you believe? Explain.

20 _____ • _____

_____

_____

_____

20 _____ • _____

_____

_____

_____

20 _____ • _____

_____

_____

_____

20 _____ • _____

_____

_____

_____

20 _____ • _____

_____

_____

_____

What nagging thought
is in the back of your mind?

20 _____ • _____

_____

_____

_____

20 _____ • _____

_____

_____

_____

20 _____ • _____

_____

_____

_____

20 _____ • _____

_____

_____

_____

20 _____ • _____

_____

_____

_____

AUGUST

Are you prioritizing anything above
your relationship with God?

20 _____ • _____

_____

_____

_____

20 _____ • _____

_____

_____

_____

20 _____ • _____

_____

_____

_____

20 _____ • _____

_____

_____

_____

20 _____ • _____

_____

_____

_____

AUGUST

What do you need to tell yourself today?

20 _____ • _____

_____

_____

_____

20 _____ • _____

_____

_____

_____

20 _____ • _____

_____

_____

_____

20 _____ • _____

_____

_____

_____

20 _____ • _____

_____

_____

_____

AUGUST

What book of the Bible would you
like to understand better?

20 _____ • _____

_____

_____

_____

20 _____ • _____

_____

_____

_____

20 _____ • _____

_____

_____

_____

20 _____ • _____

_____

_____

_____

20 _____ • _____

_____

_____

_____

AUGUST

When do you feel most like yourself?

20 _____ • _____

_____

_____

_____

20 _____ • _____

_____

_____

_____

20 _____ • _____

_____

_____

_____

20 _____ • _____

_____

_____

_____

20 _____ • _____

_____

_____

_____

AUGUST

What isn't getting done?

20 _____ • _____

_____

_____

_____

20 _____ • _____

_____

_____

_____

20 _____ • _____

_____

_____

_____

20 _____ • _____

_____

_____

_____

20 _____ • _____

_____

_____

_____

How can you encourage a pastor
or ministry leader this week?

20 _____ • _____
_____
_____
_____

20 _____ • _____
_____
_____
_____

20 _____ • _____
_____
_____
_____

20 _____ • _____
_____
_____
_____

20 _____ • _____
_____
_____
_____

AUGUST

What act of kindness did you
demonstrate or witness today?

20 _____ • _____

_____

_____

_____

20 _____ • _____

_____

_____

_____

20 _____ • _____

_____

_____

_____

20 _____ • _____

_____

_____

_____

20 _____ • _____

_____

_____

_____

What character trait in yourself
will you thank God for today?

20 _____ • _____

_____

_____

_____

20 _____ • _____

_____

_____

_____

20 _____ • _____

_____

_____

_____

20 _____ • _____

_____

_____

_____

20 _____ • _____

_____

_____

_____

AUGUST

What are you doing that's working for you?

20 _____ • _____

20 _____ • _____

20 _____ • _____

20 _____ • _____

20 _____ • _____

What are you chasing at this moment?

20 _____ • _____

_____

_____

_____

20 _____ • _____

_____

_____

_____

20 _____ • _____

_____

_____

_____

20 _____ • _____

_____

_____

_____

20 _____ • _____

_____

_____

_____

AUGUST

What was the last dream you had
that you can remember?

20 _____ • _____

_____

_____

_____

20 _____ • _____

_____

_____

_____

20 _____ • _____

_____

_____

_____

20 _____ • _____

_____

_____

_____

20 _____ • _____

_____

_____

_____

19

What are you working on in your faith?

20 _____ • _____

_____

_____

_____

20 _____ • _____

_____

_____

_____

20 _____ • _____

_____

_____

_____

20 _____ • _____

_____

_____

_____

20 _____ • _____

_____

_____

_____

AUGUST

What's coming up that you are dreading?

20 _____ • _____

_____

_____

_____

20 _____ • _____

_____

_____

_____

20 _____ • _____

_____

_____

_____

20 _____ • _____

_____

_____

_____

20 _____ • _____

_____

_____

_____

AUGUST

If God could do a miracle in one area
of your life, what would it be?

20 _____ • _____

_____

_____

_____

20 _____ • _____

_____

_____

_____

20 _____ • _____

_____

_____

_____

20 _____ • _____

_____

_____

_____

20 _____ • _____

_____

_____

_____

AUGUST

What hurts today?

20 ___ • _____
_____
_____
_____

20 ___ • _____
_____
_____
_____

20 ___ • _____
_____
_____
_____

20 ___ • _____
_____
_____
_____

20 ___ • _____
_____
_____
_____

AUGUST

Who brought you joy today?

20 _____ • _____

_____

_____

_____

20 _____ • _____

_____

_____

_____

20 _____ • _____

_____

_____

_____

20 _____ • _____

_____

_____

_____

20 _____ • _____

_____

_____

_____

AUGUST

Do you believe that God loves you?

20 _____ • _____

_____

_____

_____

20 _____ • _____

_____

_____

_____

20 _____ • _____

_____

_____

_____

20 _____ • _____

_____

_____

_____

20 _____ • _____

_____

_____

_____

AUGUST

Who is on your heart in this moment?

20 ___ • _____
_____
_____
_____

20 ___ • _____
_____
_____
_____

20 ___ • _____
_____
_____
_____

20 ___ • _____
_____
_____
_____

20 ___ • _____
_____
_____
_____

AUGUST

What expectations do you have
of those around you?

20 _____ • _____

_____

_____

_____

20 _____ • _____

_____

_____

_____

20 _____ • _____

_____

_____

_____

20 _____ • _____

_____

_____

_____

20 _____ • _____

_____

_____

_____

27

AUGUST

What prayer do you most want answered?

20 _____ • _____

_____

_____

_____

20 _____ • _____

_____

_____

_____

20 _____ • _____

_____

_____

_____

20 _____ • _____

_____

_____

_____

20 _____ • _____

_____

_____

_____

AUGUST

Who do you miss the most?

20 _____ • _____

_____

_____

_____

20 _____ • _____

_____

_____

_____

20 _____ • _____

_____

_____

_____

20 _____ • _____

_____

_____

_____

20 _____ • _____

_____

_____

_____

Where do you wish you could be right now?

20 _____ • _____

_____

_____

_____

20 _____ • _____

_____

_____

_____

20 _____ • _____

_____

_____

_____

20 _____ • _____

_____

_____

_____

20 _____ • _____

_____

_____

_____

AUGUST

What is your craziest aspiration?

20 _____ • _____

_____

_____

_____

20 _____ • _____

_____

_____

_____

20 _____ • _____

_____

_____

_____

20 _____ • _____

_____

_____

_____

20 _____ • _____

_____

_____

_____

When was the last time you had
an inspiring conversation?

20 _____ • _____
_____
_____
_____

20 _____ • _____
_____
_____
_____

20 _____ • _____
_____
_____
_____

20 _____ • _____
_____
_____
_____

20 _____ • _____
_____
_____
_____

SEPTEMBER

How could today have been better?

20 ____ • _____

_____

_____

_____

20 ____ • _____

_____

_____

_____

20 ____ • _____

_____

_____

_____

20 ____ • _____

_____

_____

_____

20 ____ • _____

_____

_____

_____

SEPTEMBER

What has caused you to feel
the nearness of God?

20 _____ • _____

_____

_____

_____

20 _____ • _____

_____

_____

_____

20 _____ • _____

_____

_____

_____

20 _____ • _____

_____

_____

_____

20 _____ • _____

_____

_____

_____

SEPTEMBER

What is the best gift
you've gotten in the past year?

20 _____ • _____

20 _____ • _____

20 _____ • _____

20 _____ • _____

20 _____ • _____

SEPTEMBER

How do you want to be remembered?

20 _____ • _____

_____

_____

_____

20 _____ • _____

_____

_____

_____

20 _____ • _____

_____

_____

_____

20 _____ • _____

_____

_____

_____

20 _____ • _____

_____

_____

_____

5

What do you have trouble believing God can do?

20 _____ • _____

_____

_____

_____

20 _____ • _____

_____

_____

_____

20 _____ • _____

_____

_____

_____

20 _____ • _____

_____

_____

_____

20 _____ • _____

_____

_____

_____

What quality do you most admire in others?

20 _____ • _____

_____

_____

_____

20 _____ • _____

_____

_____

_____

20 _____ • _____

_____

_____

_____

20 _____ • _____

_____

_____

_____

20 _____ • _____

_____

_____

_____

SEPTEMBER

If you could ask God for one
thing today, what would it be?

20 ____ • _____
_____
_____
_____

20 ____ • _____
_____
_____
_____

20 ____ • _____
_____
_____
_____

20 ____ • _____
_____
_____
_____

20 ____ • _____
_____
_____
_____

SEPTEMBER

What do you have no patience for?

20 _____ • _____

_____

_____

_____

20 _____ • _____

_____

_____

_____

20 _____ • _____

_____

_____

_____

20 _____ • _____

_____

_____

_____

20 _____ • _____

_____

_____

_____

Write out one of your favorite Bible verses.

20 _____ • _____

_____

_____

_____

20 _____ • _____

_____

_____

_____

20 _____ • _____

_____

_____

_____

20 _____ • _____

_____

_____

_____

20 _____ • _____

_____

_____

_____

SEPTEMBER

What intimidates you?

20 ___ • _____

_____

_____

_____

20 ___ • _____

_____

_____

_____

20 ___ • _____

_____

_____

_____

20 ___ • _____

_____

_____

_____

20 ___ • _____

_____

_____

_____

When were you last in a church
building or spiritual gathering place?
Why were you there?

20 _____ • _____

_____

_____

_____

20 _____ • _____

_____

_____

_____

20 _____ • _____

_____

_____

_____

20 _____ • _____

_____

_____

_____

20 _____ • _____

_____

_____

_____

SEPTEMBER

What was the best celebration
you've been to recently?

20 _____ • _____

_____

_____

_____

20 _____ • _____

_____

_____

_____

20 _____ • _____

_____

_____

_____

20 _____ • _____

_____

_____

_____

20 _____ • _____

_____

_____

_____

SEPTEMBER

What random act of kindness can you do today?

20 _____ • _____

_____

_____

_____

20 _____ • _____

_____

_____

_____

20 _____ • _____

_____

_____

_____

20 _____ • _____

_____

_____

_____

20 _____ • _____

_____

_____

_____

SEPTEMBER

What is God asking you to do that scares you?

20 _____ • _____

_____

_____

_____

20 _____ • _____

_____

_____

_____

20 _____ • _____

_____

_____

_____

20 _____ • _____

_____

_____

_____

20 _____ • _____

_____

_____

_____

Who do you wish you
had a better relationship with?

20 _____ • _____

_____

_____

_____

20 _____ • _____

_____

_____

_____

20 _____ • _____

_____

_____

_____

20 _____ • _____

_____

_____

_____

20 _____ • _____

_____

_____

_____

SEPTEMBER

Who inspires you?

20 _____ • _____

_____

_____

_____

20 _____ • _____

_____

_____

_____

20 _____ • _____

_____

_____

_____

20 _____ • _____

_____

_____

_____

20 _____ • _____

_____

_____

_____

Where do you need to change
course in your life?

20 _____ • _____

_____

_____

_____

20 _____ • _____

_____

_____

_____

20 _____ • _____

_____

_____

_____

20 _____ • _____

_____

_____

_____

20 _____ • _____

_____

_____

_____

SEPTEMBER

What worries you the most right now?

20 _____ • _____

_____

_____

_____

20 _____ • _____

_____

_____

_____

20 _____ • _____

_____

_____

_____

20 _____ • _____

_____

_____

_____

20 _____ • _____

_____

_____

_____

What friend can you turn to
when you need someone?

20 _____ • _____

_____

_____

_____

20 _____ • _____

_____

_____

_____

20 _____ • _____

_____

_____

_____

20 _____ • _____

_____

_____

_____

20 _____ • _____

_____

_____

_____

SEPTEMBER

What's the best part of your life right now?

20 _____ • _____

_____

_____

20 _____ • _____

_____

_____

20 _____ • _____

_____

_____

20 _____ • _____

_____

_____

20 _____ • _____

_____

_____

Who are three of your favorite
preachers, teachers, or speakers?

20 _____ • _____

_____

_____

_____

20 _____ • _____

_____

_____

_____

20 _____ • _____

_____

_____

_____

20 _____ • _____

_____

_____

_____

20 _____ • _____

_____

_____

_____

SEPTEMBER

Did you try something new today?

20 _____ • _____

_____

_____

_____

20 _____ • _____

_____

_____

_____

20 _____ • _____

_____

_____

_____

20 _____ • _____

_____

_____

_____

20 _____ • _____

_____

_____

_____

What are your hopes for this fall?

20 _____ • _____

_____

_____

_____

20 _____ • _____

_____

_____

_____

20 _____ • _____

_____

_____

_____

20 _____ • _____

_____

_____

_____

20 _____ • _____

_____

_____

_____

SEPTEMBER

What is one of your favorite
New Testament stories or verses?

20 _____ • _____

_____

_____

_____

20 _____ • _____

_____

_____

_____

20 _____ • _____

_____

_____

_____

20 _____ • _____

_____

_____

_____

20 _____ • _____

_____

_____

_____

What do you need to forgive yourself for?

20 ___ • _____

_____

_____

_____

20 ___ • _____

_____

_____

_____

20 ___ • _____

_____

_____

_____

20 ___ • _____

_____

_____

_____

20 ___ • _____

_____

_____

_____

SEPTEMBER

Have you ever witnessed a miracle?

20 ____ • _____

_____

_____

_____

20 ____ • _____

_____

_____

_____

20 ____ • _____

_____

_____

_____

20 ____ • _____

_____

_____

_____

20 ____ • _____

_____

_____

_____

What do you wish you could have
told yourself five years ago?

20 _____ • _____
_____
_____
_____

20 _____ • _____
_____
_____
_____

20 _____ • _____
_____
_____
_____

20 _____ • _____
_____
_____
_____

20 _____ • _____
_____
_____
_____

SEPTEMBER

What do you need to do differently?

20 _____ • _____

20 _____ • _____

20 _____ • _____

20 _____ • _____

20 _____ • _____

SEPTEMBER

What decision are you glad you made?

20 ____ • _____

_____

_____

_____

20 ____ • _____

_____

_____

_____

20 ____ • _____

_____

_____

_____

20 ____ • _____

_____

_____

_____

20 ____ • _____

_____

_____

_____

SEPTEMBER

What obstacle is keeping you
from your spiritual goal?

20 _____ • _____

_____

_____

_____

20 _____ • _____

_____

_____

_____

20 _____ • _____

_____

_____

_____

20 _____ • _____

_____

_____

_____

20 _____ • _____

_____

_____

_____

OCTOBER

OCTOBER

What is the most moving thing a
friend has done for you recently?

20 ____ • _____

_____

_____

_____

20 ____ • _____

_____

_____

_____

20 ____ • _____

_____

_____

_____

20 ____ • _____

_____

_____

_____

20 ____ • _____

_____

_____

_____

OCTOBER

What can't you forget?

20 ____ • _____

_____

_____

_____

20 ____ • _____

_____

_____

_____

20 ____ • _____

_____

_____

_____

20 ____ • _____

_____

_____

_____

20 ____ • _____

_____

_____

_____

OCTOBER

What do you wish more
people knew about you?

20 _____ • _____

_____

_____

_____

20 _____ • _____

_____

_____

_____

20 _____ • _____

_____

_____

_____

20 _____ • _____

_____

_____

_____

20 _____ • _____

_____

_____

_____

OCTOBER

What do you feel grateful for today?

20 _____ • _____

_____

_____

_____

20 _____ • _____

_____

_____

_____

20 _____ • _____

_____

_____

_____

20 _____ • _____

_____

_____

_____

20 _____ • _____

_____

_____

_____

OCTOBER

Today I needed more _____.

20 ___ • _____

_____

_____

_____

20 ___ • _____

_____

_____

_____

20 ___ • _____

_____

_____

_____

20 ___ • _____

_____

_____

_____

20 ___ • _____

_____

_____

_____

20 _____ • _____

_____

_____

_____

20 _____ • _____

_____

_____

_____

20 _____ • _____

_____

_____

_____

20 _____ • _____

_____

_____

_____

20 _____ • _____

_____

_____

_____

OCTOBER

What Bible verse do you
resonate with right now?

20 ___ • _____

_____

_____

_____

20 ___ • _____

_____

_____

_____

20 ___ • _____

_____

_____

_____

20 ___ • _____

_____

_____

_____

20 ___ • _____

_____

_____

_____

OCTOBER

What are you currently reading?

20 _____ • _____

_____

_____

_____

20 _____ • _____

_____

_____

_____

20 _____ • _____

_____

_____

_____

20 _____ • _____

_____

_____

_____

20 _____ • _____

_____

_____

_____

OCTOBER

What is something you're letting
fear get in the way of?

20 _____ • _____

_____

_____

_____

20 _____ • _____

_____

_____

_____

20 _____ • _____

_____

_____

_____

20 _____ • _____

_____

_____

_____

20 _____ • _____

_____

_____

_____

How does it make you feel to know
that God knows everything about you?

20 _____ • _____

_____

_____

_____

20 _____ • _____

_____

_____

_____

20 _____ • _____

_____

_____

_____

20 _____ • _____

_____

_____

_____

20 _____ • _____

_____

_____

_____

OCTOBER

What was the last thing
you taught someone to do?

20 _____ • _____

_____

_____

_____

20 _____ • _____

_____

_____

_____

20 _____ • _____

_____

_____

_____

20 _____ • _____

_____

_____

_____

20 _____ • _____

_____

_____

_____

OCTOBER

Who is God asking you to show love to?

20 _____ • _____

_____

_____

_____

20 _____ • _____

_____

_____

_____

20 _____ • _____

_____

_____

_____

20 _____ • _____

_____

_____

_____

20 _____ • _____

_____

_____

_____

OCTOBER

What do you want to forget?

20 _____ • _____

_____

_____

_____

20 _____ • _____

_____

_____

_____

20 _____ • _____

_____

_____

20 _____ • _____

_____

_____

20 _____ • _____

_____

_____

_____

What would the most restful weekend
imaginable look like to you?

20 _____ • _____

_____

_____

_____

20 _____ • _____

_____

_____

_____

20 _____ • _____

_____

_____

_____

20 _____ • _____

_____

_____

_____

20 _____ • _____

_____

_____

_____

OCTOBER

Who has encouraged you
in your faith journey?

20 _____ • _____

_____

_____

_____

20 _____ • _____

_____

_____

_____

20 _____ • _____

_____

_____

_____

20 _____ • _____

_____

_____

_____

20 _____ • _____

_____

_____

_____

What do you like about today's weather?

20 _____ • _____

_____

_____

_____

20 _____ • _____

_____

_____

_____

20 _____ • _____

_____

_____

_____

20 _____ • _____

_____

_____

_____

20 _____ • _____

_____

_____

_____

OCTOBER

What aspect of God brought hope to you today?

20 _____ • _____

_____

_____

_____

20 _____ • _____

_____

_____

_____

20 _____ • _____

_____

_____

_____

20 _____ • _____

_____

_____

_____

20 _____ • _____

_____

_____

_____

OCTOBER

How can you encourage your
friend, spouse, or child today?

20 _____ • _____
_____
_____
_____

20 _____ • _____
_____
_____
_____

20 _____ • _____
_____
_____
_____

20 _____ • _____
_____
_____
_____

20 _____ • _____
_____
_____
_____

OCTOBER

What situation would you have handled
differently, given another opportunity?

20 _____ • _____

_____

_____

_____

20 _____ • _____

_____

_____

_____

20 _____ • _____

_____

_____

_____

20 _____ • _____

_____

_____

_____

20 _____ • _____

_____

_____

_____

OCTOBER

If you could change something
about yourself, what would it be?

20 ____ • _____

20 ____ • _____

20 ____ • _____

20 ____ • _____

20 ____ • _____

OCTOBER

Do you feel more comfortable
alone or in big groups?

20 ___ • _____

_____

_____

_____

20 ___ • _____

_____

_____

_____

20 ___ • _____

_____

_____

_____

20 ___ • _____

_____

_____

_____

20 ___ • _____

_____

_____

_____

OCTOBER

When God looks at you, He sees _____.
When you look at yourself, you see _____.

20 ___ • _____

_____

_____

_____

20 ___ • _____

_____

_____

_____

20 ___ • _____

_____

_____

_____

20 ___ • _____

_____

_____

_____

20 ___ • _____

_____

_____

_____

OCTOBER

What motivated you today?

20 _____ • _____

_____

_____

_____

20 _____ • _____

_____

_____

_____

20 _____ • _____

_____

_____

_____

20 _____ • _____

_____

_____

_____

20 _____ • _____

_____

_____

_____

What have you been studying
in the Bible recently?

20 ____ • _____
_____
_____
_____

20 ____ • _____
_____
_____
_____

20 ____ • _____
_____
_____
_____

20 ____ • _____
_____
_____
_____

20 ____ • _____
_____
_____
_____

OCTOBER

How can you encourage a friend today?

20 _____ • _____

_____

_____

_____

20 _____ • _____

_____

_____

_____

20 _____ • _____

_____

_____

_____

20 _____ • _____

_____

_____

_____

20 _____ • _____

_____

_____

_____

What do you have a hard time leaving as is?

20 _____ • _____

_____

_____

_____

20 _____ • _____

_____

_____

_____

20 _____ • _____

_____

_____

_____

20 _____ • _____

_____

_____

_____

20 _____ • _____

_____

_____

_____

What attribute do you appreciate in others
because you don't have it yourself?

20 ____ • _____

_____

_____

_____

20 ____ • _____

_____

_____

_____

20 ____ • _____

_____

_____

_____

20 ____ • _____

_____

_____

_____

20 ____ • _____

_____

_____

_____

What is one way you can be a
better servant to others?

20 _____ • _____

_____

_____

_____

20 _____ • _____

_____

_____

_____

20 _____ • _____

_____

_____

_____

20 _____ • _____

_____

_____

_____

20 _____ • _____

_____

_____

_____

OCTOBER

What is missing in your life?

20 _____ • _____

_____

_____

_____

20 _____ • _____

_____

_____

_____

20 _____ • _____

_____

_____

_____

20 _____ • _____

_____

_____

_____

20 _____ • _____

_____

_____

_____

OCTOBER

Who are you praying for today?

20 _____ • _____

_____

_____

_____

20 _____ • _____

_____

_____

_____

20 _____ • _____

_____

_____

_____

20 _____ • _____

_____

_____

_____

20 _____ • _____

_____

_____

_____

OCTOBER

What's a recent movie you've watched
that showed grace?

20 ____ • _____

_____

_____

_____

20 ____ • _____

_____

_____

_____

20 ____ • _____

_____

_____

_____

20 ____ • _____

_____

_____

_____

20 ____ • _____

_____

_____

_____

NOVEMBER

NOVEMBER

Who are you holding a grudge against
that you need to ask forgiveness for?

20 _____ • _____

_____

_____

_____

20 _____ • _____

_____

_____

_____

20 _____ • _____

_____

_____

_____

20 _____ • _____

_____

_____

_____

20 _____ • _____

_____

_____

_____

NOVEMBER

Are you pleased with your faith?

20 ___ • _____

_____

_____

_____

20 ___ • _____

_____

_____

_____

20 ___ • _____

_____

_____

_____

20 ___ • _____

_____

_____

_____

20 ___ • _____

_____

_____

_____

NOVEMBER

What is your motto?

20 ___ • _____

_____

_____

_____

20 ___ • _____

_____

_____

_____

20 ___ • _____

_____

_____

_____

20 ___ • _____

_____

_____

_____

20 ___ • _____

_____

_____

_____

20 _____ • _____

_____

_____

_____

20 _____ • _____

_____

_____

_____

20 _____ • _____

_____

_____

_____

20 _____ • _____

_____

_____

_____

20 _____ • _____

_____

_____

_____

NOVEMBER

What was the last thing that brought you joy?

20 _____ • _____

_____

_____

_____

20 _____ • _____

_____

_____

_____

20 _____ • _____

_____

_____

_____

20 _____ • _____

_____

_____

_____

20 _____ • _____

_____

_____

_____

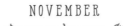

What is something out of the ordinary
you can celebrate or be thankful for today?

20 _____ • _____

_____

_____

_____

20 _____ • _____

_____

_____

_____

20 _____ • _____

_____

_____

_____

20 _____ • _____

_____

_____

_____

20 _____ • _____

_____

_____

_____

NOVEMBER

What inspired you today?

20 ____ • _____

_____

_____

_____

20 ____ • _____

_____

_____

_____

20 ____ • _____

_____

_____

_____

20 ____ • _____

_____

_____

_____

20 ____ • _____

_____

_____

_____

NOVEMBER

What do you want to postpone?

20 ___ • _____

_____

_____

_____

20 ___ • _____

_____

_____

_____

20 ___ • _____

_____

_____

_____

20 ___ • _____

_____

_____

_____

20 ___ • _____

_____

_____

_____

NOVEMBER

What is/was your typical Sunday/Sabbath
routine (either now or in your childhood)?

20 _____ • _____

_____

_____

_____

20 _____ • _____

_____

_____

_____

20 _____ • _____

_____

_____

_____

20 _____ • _____

_____

_____

_____

20 _____ • _____

_____

_____

_____

NOVEMBER

What is the hardest question for you to answer?

20 _____ • _____

_____

_____

_____

20 _____ • _____

_____

_____

_____

20 _____ • _____

_____

_____

_____

20 _____ • _____

_____

_____

_____

20 _____ • _____

_____

_____

_____

NOVEMBER

What can you thank God for today?

20 _____ • _____

_____

_____

_____

20 _____ • _____

_____

_____

_____

20 _____ • _____

_____

_____

_____

20 _____ • _____

_____

_____

_____

20 _____ • _____

_____

_____

_____

NOVEMBER

On a scale of one to ten,
how sad are you? Why?

20 ____ • _____

_____

_____

_____

20 ____ • _____

_____

_____

_____

20 ____ • _____

_____

_____

_____

20 ____ • _____

_____

_____

_____

20 ____ • _____

_____

_____

_____

NOVEMBER

What prayer have you seen
answered recently?

20 _____ • _____

_____

_____

_____

20 _____ • _____

_____

_____

_____

20 _____ • _____

_____

_____

_____

20 _____ • _____

_____

_____

_____

20 _____ • _____

_____

_____

_____

What keeps you from showing
hospitality to others?

20 ____ • _____
_____
_____
_____

20 ____ • _____
_____
_____
_____

20 ____ • _____
_____
_____
_____

20 ____ • _____
_____
_____
_____

20 ____ • _____
_____
_____
_____

NOVEMBER

Who are the most important people
in your life right now?

20 ___ • _____

_____

_____

_____

20 ___ • _____

_____

_____

_____

20 ___ • _____

_____

_____

_____

20 ___ • _____

_____

_____

_____

20 ___ • _____

_____

_____

_____

NOVEMBER

What Bible verse speaks best
to your challenges right now?

20 ___ • _____

_____

_____

_____

20 ___ • _____

_____

_____

_____

20 ___ • _____

_____

_____

_____

20 ___ • _____

_____

_____

_____

20 ___ • _____

_____

_____

_____

NOVEMBER

Who should you talk to today?

20 _____ • _____

_____

_____

_____

20 _____ • _____

_____

_____

_____

20 _____ • _____

_____

_____

_____

20 _____ • _____

_____

_____

_____

20 _____ • _____

_____

_____

_____

NOVEMBER

If you could be the best
at anything, what would it be?

20 ___ • _____

_____

_____

_____

20 ___ • _____

_____

_____

_____

20 ___ • _____

_____

_____

_____

20 ___ • _____

_____

_____

_____

20 ___ • _____

_____

_____

_____

NOVEMBER

In what circumstances are you able
to put your gifts to best use?

20 ____ • _____

_____

_____

20 ____ • _____

_____

_____

20 ____ • _____

_____

_____

20 ____ • _____

_____

_____

20 ____ • _____

_____

_____

NOVEMBER

The most unusual thing about
today was _____.

20 ____ • _____
_____
_____
_____

20 ____ • _____
_____
_____
_____

20 ____ • _____
_____
_____
_____

20 ____ • _____
_____
_____
_____

20 ____ • _____
_____
_____
_____

NOVEMBER

What is one thing you want to do for your
community by this time next year?

20 _____ • _____

_____

_____

_____

20 _____ • _____

_____

_____

_____

20 _____ • _____

_____

_____

_____

20 _____ • _____

_____

_____

_____

20 _____ • _____

_____

_____

_____

NOVEMBER

Who would you like to be more like?

20 _____ • _____

_____

_____

_____

20 _____ • _____

_____

_____

_____

20 _____ • _____

_____

_____

_____

20 _____ • _____

_____

_____

_____

20 _____ • _____

_____

_____

_____

NOVEMBER

What nonphysical thing have you
held on to for too long?

20 ___ • _____

_____

_____

_____

20 ___ • _____

_____

_____

_____

20 ___ • _____

_____

_____

_____

20 ___ • _____

_____

_____

_____

20 ___ • _____

_____

_____

_____

What is one way you can serve
those around you today?

20 _____ • _____

_____

_____

_____

20 _____ • _____

_____

_____

_____

20 _____ • _____

_____

_____

_____

20 _____ • _____

_____

_____

_____

20 _____ • _____

_____

_____

_____

NOVEMBER

If you could ask God one question face
to face today, what would it be?

20 _____ • _____

_____

_____

_____

20 _____ • _____

_____

_____

_____

20 _____ • _____

_____

_____

_____

20 _____ • _____

_____

_____

_____

20 _____ • _____

_____

_____

_____

NOVEMBER

Why do you (or don't you) go to church?

20 _____ • _____

_____

_____

_____

20 _____ • _____

_____

_____

_____

20 _____ • _____

_____

_____

_____

20 _____ • _____

_____

_____

_____

20 _____ • _____

_____

_____

_____

NOVEMBER

What is the most sacrificial thing
you've done this year for a friend?

20 _____ • _____

_____

_____

_____

20 _____ • _____

_____

_____

_____

20 _____ • _____

_____

_____

_____

20 _____ • _____

_____

_____

_____

20 _____ • _____

_____

_____

_____

NOVEMBER

What is your best nonphysical attribute?

20 ____ • _____
_____
_____
_____

20 ____ • _____
_____
_____
_____

20 ____ • _____
_____
_____
_____

20 ____ • _____
_____
_____
_____

20 ____ • _____
_____
_____
_____

NOVEMBER

What was peaceful about today?

20 ___ • _____

_____

_____

_____

20 ___ • _____

_____

_____

_____

20 ___ • _____

_____

_____

_____

20 ___ • _____

_____

_____

_____

20 ___ • _____

_____

_____

_____

20 _____ • _____
_____
_____
_____

20 _____ • _____
_____
_____
_____

20 _____ • _____
_____
_____
_____

20 _____ • _____
_____
_____
_____

20 _____ • _____
_____
_____
_____

DECEMBER

DECEMBER

What faith-related book
are you currently reading?

20 _____ • _____

20 _____ • _____

20 _____ • _____

20 _____ • _____

20 _____ • _____

DECEMBER

Who can you help grow in their faith?

20 _____ • _____

_____

_____

_____

20 _____ • _____

_____

_____

_____

20 _____ • _____

_____

_____

_____

20 _____ • _____

_____

_____

_____

20 _____ • _____

_____

_____

_____

What is something you're thankful for
but tend to take for granted?

20 ___ • _____

_____

_____

_____

20 ___ • _____

_____

_____

_____

20 ___ • _____

_____

_____

_____

20 ___ • _____

_____

_____

_____

20 ___ • _____

_____

_____

_____

DECEMBER

What was the last personal
letter you wrote?

20 _____ • _____

_____

_____

_____

20 _____ • _____

_____

_____

_____

20 _____ • _____

_____

_____

_____

20 _____ • _____

_____

_____

_____

20 _____ • _____

_____

_____

_____

DECEMBER

What Bible verse helps you
get through hard times?

20 _____ • _____

_____

_____

_____

20 _____ • _____

_____

_____

_____

20 _____ • _____

_____

_____

_____

20 _____ • _____

_____

_____

_____

20 _____ • _____

_____

_____

_____

DECEMBER

What do you tell yourself most often?

20 _____ • _____

_____

_____

_____

20 _____ • _____

_____

_____

_____

20 _____ • _____

_____

_____

_____

20 _____ • _____

_____

_____

_____

20 _____ • _____

_____

_____

_____

20 ___ • _____

_____

_____

_____

20 ___ • _____

_____

_____

_____

20 ___ • _____

_____

_____

_____

20 ___ • _____

_____

_____

_____

20 ___ • _____

_____

_____

_____

If you could create and pass a
new law, what would it be?

20 _____ • _____

_____

_____

_____

20 _____ • _____

_____

_____

_____

20 _____ • _____

_____

_____

_____

20 _____ • _____

_____

_____

_____

20 _____ • _____

_____

_____

_____

20 _____ • _____

_____

_____

_____

20 _____ • _____

_____

_____

_____

20 _____ • _____

_____

_____

_____

20 _____ • _____

_____

_____

_____

20 _____ • _____

_____

_____

_____

DECEMBER

How have your opinions shifted this year?

20 _____ • _____

_____

_____

_____

_____

20 _____ • _____

_____

_____

_____

_____

20 _____ • _____

_____

_____

_____

_____

20 _____ • _____

_____

_____

_____

_____

20 _____ • _____

_____

_____

_____

_____

DECEMBER

It still surprises me that _____.

20 ___ • _____

_____

_____

_____

20 ___ • _____

_____

_____

_____

20 ___ • _____

_____

_____

_____

20 ___ • _____

_____

_____

_____

20 ___ • _____

_____

_____

_____

DECEMBER

What's the most valuable thing you own?

20 _____ • _____
_____
_____
_____

20 _____ • _____
_____
_____
_____

20 _____ • _____
_____
_____
_____

20 _____ • _____
_____
_____
_____

20 _____ • _____
_____
_____
_____

What song or hymn perfectly
captures your mood today?

20 _____ • _____

_____

_____

_____

20 _____ • _____

_____

_____

_____

20 _____ • _____

_____

_____

_____

20 _____ • _____

_____

_____

_____

20 _____ • _____

_____

_____

_____

Who could you surprise with a card
or inexpensive gift this Christmas?

20 _____ • _____

_____

_____

_____

20 _____ • _____

_____

_____

_____

20 _____ • _____

_____

_____

_____

20 _____ • _____

_____

_____

_____

20 _____ • _____

_____

_____

_____

What lie from the Enemy
do you believe about yourself?

20 _____ • _____

_____

_____

_____

20 _____ • _____

_____

_____

_____

20 _____ • _____

_____

_____

_____

20 _____ • _____

_____

_____

_____

20 _____ • _____

_____

_____

_____

DECEMBER

How have you helped another person today?

20 _____ • _____

_____

_____

_____

20 _____ • _____

_____

_____

_____

20 _____ • _____

_____

_____

_____

20 _____ • _____

_____

_____

_____

20 _____ • _____

_____

_____

_____

What gift have you been excited to give?

20 _____ • _____

_____

_____

_____

20 _____ • _____

_____

_____

_____

20 _____ • _____

_____

_____

_____

20 _____ • _____

_____

_____

_____

20 _____ • _____

_____

_____

_____

DECEMBER

What do you need to remember today?

20 ____ • _____

_____

_____

_____

20 ____ • _____

_____

_____

_____

20 ____ • _____

_____

_____

_____

20 ____ • _____

_____

_____

_____

20 ____ • _____

_____

_____

_____

What books of the Bible have you never read?

20 _____ • _____

_____

_____

_____

20 _____ • _____

_____

_____

20 _____ • _____

_____

_____

20 _____ • _____

_____

_____

20 _____ • _____

_____

_____

DECEMBER

If you could do anything at all today,
what would it be?

20 ____ • _____

_____

_____

20 ____ • _____

_____

_____

20 ____ • _____

_____

_____

20 ____ • _____

_____

_____

20 ____ • _____

_____

_____

What are the first words that come
to mind when you think of God?

20 _____ • _____

_____

_____

_____

20 _____ • _____

_____

_____

_____

20 _____ • _____

_____

_____

_____

20 _____ • _____

_____

_____

_____

20 _____ • _____

_____

_____

_____

DECEMBER

Who is your closest friend, and how
can you pray for that person right now?

20 _____ • _____

_____

_____

_____

20 _____ • _____

_____

_____

_____

20 _____ • _____

_____

_____

_____

20 _____ • _____

_____

_____

_____

20 _____ • _____

_____

_____

_____

What is a holiday memory that makes you smile?

20 _____ • _____

_____

_____

_____

20 _____ • _____

_____

_____

_____

20 _____ • _____

_____

_____

_____

20 _____ • _____

_____

_____

_____

20 _____ • _____

_____

_____

_____

DECEMBER

What recent situation required
you to exercise patience?

20 _____ • _____

_____

_____

_____

20 _____ • _____

_____

_____

_____

20 _____ • _____

_____

_____

_____

20 _____ • _____

_____

_____

_____

20 _____ • _____

_____

_____

_____

What happened today
that you want to remember?

20 ____ • _____

_____

_____

_____

20 ____ • _____

_____

_____

_____

20 ____ • _____

_____

_____

_____

20 ____ • _____

_____

_____

_____

20 ____ • _____

_____

_____

_____

DECEMBER

What is your favorite psalm and why?

20 _____ • _____

_____

_____

_____

20 _____ • _____

_____

_____

_____

20 _____ • _____

_____

_____

_____

20 _____ • _____

_____

_____

_____

20 _____ • _____

_____

_____

_____

What have you accomplished this year
that you are most proud of?

20 _____ • _____

_____

_____

_____

20 _____ • _____

_____

_____

_____

20 _____ • _____

_____

_____

_____

20 _____ • _____

_____

_____

_____

20 _____ • _____

_____

_____

_____

DECEMBER

What is your biggest hope for next year?

20 _____ • _____

_____

_____

_____

20 _____ • _____

_____

_____

_____

20 _____ • _____

_____

_____

_____

20 _____ • _____

_____

_____

_____

20 _____ • _____

_____

_____

_____

DECEMBER

Who do you need to call?

20 _____ • _____

_____

_____

_____

20 _____ • _____

_____

_____

_____

20 _____ • _____

_____

_____

_____

20 _____ • _____

_____

_____

_____

20 _____ • _____

_____

_____

_____

DECEMBER

What word would you
use to characterize this year?

20 ___ • _____

_____

_____

_____

20 ___ • _____

_____

_____

_____

20 ___ • _____

_____

_____

_____

20 ___ • _____

_____

_____

_____

20 ___ • _____

_____

_____

_____

What is the most important thing
you learned about yourself this year?

20 _____ • _____

_____

_____

_____

20 _____ • _____

_____

_____

_____

20 _____ • _____

_____

_____

_____

20 _____ • _____

_____

_____

_____

20 _____ • _____

_____

_____

_____

Acknowledgments

The Daily Question development team is grateful to all the individuals and departments within the Crown division and WaterBrook for their help in creating this project, in particular Pam Fogle, Karen Sherry, and Julia Wallace.

We also extend a special thank you to the following people who contributed questions for the book:

Laura Barker

Brett Benson

Christina Brandsma

Tina Constable

Kendall Davis

Alex Field

Johanna Inwood

Jamie Lapeyrolerie

Bruce Nygren

Sara Selkirk

Pam Shoup

Susan Tjaden

Laura Wright

Development Team

Kendall Davis

Jessica Lamb

Kristopher Orr

Sara Selkirk

Susan Tjaden

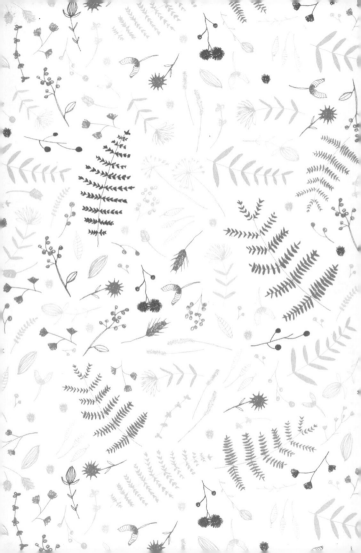